Do
AD CAMPAIGNS...
that insult your intelligence make you
GOOD 'N' MAD?
• • •

Do
TELEVISION SHOWS...
written for 6-year-old morons make you
GOOD 'N' MAD?
• • •

Do
MOVIES...
that appeal to sex perverts make you
GOOD 'N' MAD?
• • •

Do
POLITICIANS...
helping themselves, not voters, make you
GOOD 'N' MAD?
• • •

Do
ALL THE OTHER CLODS...
*bilking, conning, cheating and committing
other crimes against the public make you*
GOOD 'N' MAD?
• • •

WELL, YOU AIN'T SEEN NUTHIN' YET!

THIS BOOK WILL <u>REALLY</u> MAKE YOU...

"GOOD 'N 'MAD"!
*(Mainly because it's the worst
crime against the public ever!)*

William M. Gaines's

GOOD 'N' MAD

ALBERT B. FELDSTEIN, Editor

WARNER BOOKS

A Warner Communications Company

GOOD 'N'

MAD

GOVERNMENT

ARTIST: JACK RICKARD   WRITER: FRANK JACOBS

ADD VERSE AND CONSENT DEPT.

There's one area that the "New Frontier" hasn't attempted to change, mainly all those dull notices we get whenever the Government has something to tell us. In other words, if Federal, State and Local Governments are supposed to be friendly, then why not make their letters friendly? Just think how much more appealing all those stuffy notices and announcements would be if they were pepped up into these

GREETING CARDS

You're Getting Out!

We're happy to be telling you
Some new facts have arisen,
Which means that you won't have to do
Your last..f̲i̲v̲e̲.̲y̲e̲a̲r̲s̲.in prison;

Instead of keeping you confined
And having to support you—
We'll set you free, because we find
It's cheaper to deport you!

U.S. JUSTICE DEPT.

Thinking of You

QUIET

LIBRARY

At...2..a.m...we'll come for you
And maybe break your.....arm...in two,
And if you still won't come across,
We've other ways to show who's boss,
Like giving you the third degree,
Or seizing all your property;
To save your skin, there's just one way—
Return our..."Mother..Goose".. today!

PUBLIC LIBRARY

Thanks Loads!

Yes, thank you for your tax return;
It really was a joy to learn
That you're convinced there's so much money due you;
We really wish that we could send
A check that you could cash and spend;
Instead, we send this merry greeting to you:

On......April 10th....you will report
Before Judge..Schwartz..in..District..Court;
At..3..p..m...; you'll be the sole defendant;
The prison term that you will draw
Will show you it's against the law
To claim..a..basset..hound. as a dependent!

HAPPY VACATION!

You'll love the sights in Arkansas,
The mountains of Montana;
You'll love the wild Mardi Gras
In old Louisiana;
You'll want to try your fishing skills
In sunny Minnesota,
Then see Mt. Rushmore in the hills
Of nearby South Dakota;
In other words, you'd better plan
A U.S.A. vacation!
Because we've just refused, old man,
Your passport application!

U.S. STATE DEPT.

10

An Invitation For You

On...April 12th...please come on down
To Washington, D.C.
Where monuments of great renown
Proclaim their majesty;
It pains us that you must ignore
These highlights of our city;
'Cause, chum, you're being hauled before
A Senate sub-committee!

U.S. CONGRESS

11

Surprise!

Your Uncle Sam is building you
An eight-lane highway, nice and new;
You'll find the road is quite nearby
The property you occupy;
Your home, in fact, is in the way;
(we just condemned it yesterday)
You'd better move, and plenty fast,
'Cause in two days we start to blast!

**FEDERAL
HIGHWAY COMMISSION**

Congratulations!

We've learned the.......Buick....that you own
Was clocked at.......90....per;
And now our pleasure must be shown;
In this we all concur;
We're pleased to say we've found a way
To crown your feat so splendid;
Please be advised as of today
Your license is suspended!

STATE MOTOR VEHICLE DEPT.

To My Favorite Nephew

Because you're such a splendid lad,
Your Uncle is immensely glad
To offer you this heartfelt invitation—
I'm very sure that you'll enjoy
To hear that you are getting, boy,
A two-year, all-expenses-paid vacation!

I know it's one that you'll adore;
It beats a trip to Singapore,
To London, Paris, Cairo or Miami;
At..8..a..m.,...May..1st..we'll meet
At....102..South..14th...Street;
Please be on time; you're drafted!—

UNCLE SAMMY

We've patented the railway train,
The telephone, the monoplane,
The steamboat and the
     nuclear reactor;
We've patented the motor car,
The phonograph, the Mason jar,
The bobby pin, the doorbell,
     and the tractor;

We've patented most everything
From paper clips and balls of string
To radar screens that keep
     our land protected;
But now, alas, we're most distressed
To have to turn down your request;
Your claim to patent ..breathing.
     is rejected!

U.S. PATENT OFFICE

Sergio Aragones, MAD's newest addition, who recently arrived from "South Of The Border"—and contemplated making for it when his "MAD LOOK AT MOTORCYCLE COPS"

A MAD LOOK

ARTIST & WRITER: SERGIO ARAGONES

AT FOOTBALL

When it comes to "Driving"—Dave Berg is a master! He drives his wife to distraction . . . his kids to a frenzy . . . and his editors to drink! Therefore, it is only natural that he come up with an article to drive all you readers crazy . . . namely this look at . . .

THE
LIGHTER
SIDE OF

Well, George— How do you like **owning** one of these small foreign cars?!

I get terrific gas mileage— Repairs are inexpensive—

I can get into the smalles parking space—It turns o a dime—It hugs the roa nicely—It's great in ever respect **except one** . . .

CAR OWNERS

WRITER & ARTIST: DAVID BERG

28

Here's a **real beauty**! It's practically a **new car**! Just broken in! It's only got 11,000 miles on it . . .

USED CARS

THUMP

Why do you kick the tires?

Because guys who **know** about used cars **always** kick the tires! I don't want the dealer to think I'm a **boob,** and take **advantage** of me!

You can always tell a **boob** who doesn't know **anything** about used cars if he kicks the tires! Watch me take **advantage** of him!

SPY

VS

SPY

43

Among other things, Labor Unions today have their own doctors, their own housing developments, and the own vacation resorts. But we bet you didn't know they also have their own Field Manual. Well, they do. W found a copy outside a Union Headquarters not too long ago. And since we were exhausted from walking ar down 30 flights of steps because of an elevator operators' strike, and since we were weak from starvatio because of a milk deliverers' strike, and a meat cutters' strike and a waiters' strike, and since we ha nothing else to reäd because of a newspaper typographers' strike, we flopped down on a curb stone and peruse

THE
LABOR
UNION
MANUAL

TOP SECRET

AMERICAN ASSOCIATION
OF LABOR

A HANDBOOK OF CLASSIFIED INFORMATION
RESTRICTED TO UNION MEMBERS ONLY

ARTIST: WALLACE WOOD   WRITER: LARRY SIEGEL

INTRODUCTION

A MESSAGE FROM THE PRESIDENT
OF THE AMERICAN ASSOCIATION OF LABOR

Fellow Union Members:

Not too long ago, before Unions came into existence, Labor was ruthlessly exploited by Management. We were at the employer's mercy, and had to work long hours for pitifully low wages. Labor was helpless. This was undemocratic.

Now that Labor is Unionized and strengthened, a wonderful change has taken place. Namely, now Management is ruthlessly exploited by Labor. The employer is at *our* mercy, and we work short hours for ridiculously high wages. Management is helpless. This is true democracy.

Today, we can be justifiably proud of our accomplishments. But at the same time, we must not allow ourselves to grow complacent. Management is waging a never-ending battle against us. Somewhere on his $250,000 estate, the greedy President of General Motors is plotting and scheming. What is he plotting and scheming about? I'll tell you. He's not satisfied with his $250,000 estate. He wants more, more, *more!* He wants to be able to afford a larger, $350,000 estate . . . like mine!

What has all this got to do with an introduction to a Labor Union Manual? Frankly, very little. I just want to prove that the average Union Leader of today is no longer an uneducated, unsophisticated slob—like many of us were in the old days. I dress superbly, I am suave, and as you can see I have a beautiful vocabulary. I never allow myself to slip back into my sloppy speech habits of the past, when I was a fighting, brawling Longshoreman.

Onward with Labor—and God bless youse all.

Tough Tony Culpepper II

P.S. Carry this manual with you at all times, and study it religiously at least 4 hours every day . . . preferably on company time.

CHAPTER 1

THE FOUR BASIC KINDS OF UNIONS

Why are Unions so important to the well-being of Workers?
**IN UNIONS, THERE IS STRENGTH, IN UNIONS THERE IS PROGRESS,
IN UNIONS THERE ARE FORCES FOR DEMOCRACY AT WORK!**
Why are Unions so important to the well-being of Union Leaders?
IN UNIONS, THERE ARE DUES!
There are four basic kinds of Unions which supply these dues:

UNSKILLED LABOR UNIONS

These Unions are made up of people with no particular or important skills. The members include ditch-diggers, garbage men, street cleaners, messengers, porters and Rock 'n' Roll recording stars.

SKILLED LABOR UNIONS

These Unions consist of skilled workers such as electricians, typographers and carpenters. They are very Democratic Unions. Anybody can join these Unions. As long as you're the son of a member.

WHITE COLLAR UNIONS

These Unions consist of the nice clean people with the nice clean office jobs, including clean ambitious brown-nosing secretaries, nice well-dressed office spies, sweet shy embezzling bookkeepers, and knife-in-the-back junior executives.

THE TEAMSTERS UNION

This Union consists of all workers who don't fit in the other type Unions, and many who even do. This is a very strong Union. There is only one other Union in the world with more power and gall than the Teamsters' Union—the Soviet Union!

CHAPTER 2
COLLECTIVE BARGAINING

Whenever a Union has a grievance against Management, the only way to settle it is to sit down together and, through "Collective Bargaining", arrive at a fair and equitable solution. Here are some examples to show how Unions make use of "Collective Bargaining".

1 Management shows a profit of: **$1,000 FOR THE YEAR.**
So the Union demands: **A $1 AN HOUR INCREASE FOR ALL EMPLOYEES.**
How much would this cost Management?: **$1,000,000.**
What would this give the Union?: **$1 AN HOUR MORE FOR ALL EMPLOYEES.**
What would this leave Management?: **NOTHING.**
Management makes a fair compromise offer of: **50¢ AN HOUR.**
THE UNION MAKES A FAIR COMPROMISE OFFER OF ITS OWN.
The Union's fair compromise offer: **A STRIKE!**

2 **THE UNION HAS BEEN ON STRIKE SIX MONTHS IN AN EFFORT TO GET MANAGEMENT TO INCREASE WAGES $15 A WEEK PER MAN.**
Management offers: **A $10 A WEEK INCREASE PER MAN.**
The Union asks for: **A $12 A WEEK INCREASE PER MAN.**
Union and Management settle for: **AN $11 INCREASE.**
What does the Union do next?: **GOES ON STRIKE FOR ANOTHER INCREASE.**
Why?: **TO MAKE UP FOR WAGES LOST DURING THE SIX MONTH STRIKE.**
How long does this Merry-Go-Round go on?
IF WE PLAY OUR CARDS RIGHT, FOREVER!

3 **THE UNION WANTS A 30-HOUR WORK WEEK, A BETTER PENSION PLAN AND A SIX-WEEK-PER-YEAR PAID VACATION.**
Management offers: **A 30-HOUR WORK WEEK, A BETTER PENSION PLAN, AND A SIX-WEEK-PER-YEAR PAID VACATION.**
What does the Union do?: **GOES ON STRIKE.**
Why?: **JUST TO KEEP IN PRACTICE!**

Here is a typical man-operated elevator of the past. The elevator operator was paid $2.00 an hour to run it. But with automation taking over, the Unions have tackled the problem realistically: New jobs in new businesses will have to be found for displaced workers like these.

Here is the same elevator, which is now self-service. Thanks to a strong union, the same operator still rides it. Now, he is paid $2.00 an hour to watch the passengers press their own buttons — an example of how displaced elevator operators are going into the watch business.

CHAPTER 3
PROPER PICKETING TECHNIQUES
A—How To Picket
There are two basic methods for picketing a place of business.

THE CLOSED-RANKS CIRCLE

All picketers walk in a tight circle, screaming how cruel the employer is, what a tightwad he is, and how he has been exploiting you. Be very angry. A good way to look angry is to constantly remind yourself that you don't work at this place, that you never even met the employer, and that you were pulled out of a nice warm home by your "Local" to do picket duty here in the lousy rain.

THE LONE PICKETER

This is the "sympathy approach". A lone picketer walks back and forth looking forlorn and oppressed by Management. A sad face is effective here (also a few tears will help). A good way to look sad is to keep reminding yourself that the strike may be settled soon, and the salary you'll be making won't be nearly as much as the strike pay you've been getting from your wealthy Union "Local."

B—What To Shout While Picketing

SHOUT	USUAL EFFECTIVENESS OF SHOUT
"This place is unfair!"	Good, but overused by most picketers.
"Pass 'em by!"	See above comment.
"#$&%#!#$%&#!#!"	See above comment.
"Who said Lincoln freed the slaves?!"	A bit intellectual, but better.
"The Boss is a Fink!"	Very effective—unless the Boss's name happens to be "Fink".
"Keep Cool With Coolidge!"	Excellent! Shows that you're losing your mind because of terrible working conditions.

C—How To Handle Strike-Breakers

When a Union is picketing a plant, it is un-American for *anybody* to cross the picket line and try to enter the premises. Here are two simple but patriotic ways to handle potential strike-breakers:

THE BOUNCY-BOUNCY
CAR TECHNIQUE

THE BOUNCY-BOUNCY
MAN TECHNIQUE

If strike-breaker comes to gate in car, all picketers grab car and start bouncing it up and down. Then turn car over, smash windows, and drop match into gas tank. If driver *still* insists on going in, *threaten violence!* He has no business going into plant during a strike. He is probably a no-good rotten *"scab."*

If strike-breaker comes to gate on foot, all picketers grab him and start bouncing him up and down—preferably on hard concrete surface. Then continue to work him over as if he were a car (See The Previous Panel). He has no business going into plant during the strike. He is probably the no-good rotten *"owner."*

CHAPTER 4

YOUR UNIONS IN ACTION

One of the basic aims of Unions is to keep as many men employed as possible, regardless of the importance or necessity of their work. This is a practice which is carried out most admirably by the tremendous numbers of high-paid

BREAKDOWN OF UNIONS

GROUP I—Left to right
Piano Movers Union
Piano Stool Movers Union
Piano Tuners Union
Piano Tuner Movers Union
Piano White Key Cleaners Union
Piano Black Key Cleaners Union
Piano Crack-Between-The-Black-And-
    White-Key Cleaners Union
Standby Trombone Cleaners (In Case
    Pianist Should Suddenly Switch
    Over To That Instrument) Union
Trombone Tuners Union
Trombone Tuner Movers Union

GROUP II—Left to right
Curtain Cord Pullers Union
Knot Removers From Curtain Cords Union
Knot Makers In Curtain Cords So Knot
    Removers Will Have Something To
    Do Occasionally Union
Backstage Electricians Union
Backstage Light Bulb Replacers Union
Backstage Light Bulb Shakers To See If
    Filaments Are Broken And Bulb Has
    To Be Replaced Union
Backstage Electrician Shakers To See If
    Electrician Has Died And Has To
    Be Replaced Union

thoroughly useless Broadway Stagehand Unions. Here is a backstage shot
en at the Dick Foran Theater following a one-man performance by comedian
tor Barge, showing Union Workers that **must** be hired for each performance.

PRESENTED ABOVE

UP III—Left to right
r Movers Union

e Movers Union

ainers To Chair And Table Movers
  The Difference Between A Chair
  And A Table Union

m Clock Setters To Keep Chair And
  Table Movers From Falling Asleep
  Union

m Clock Setters To Keep Alarm Clock
  Setters Who Keep Chair And Table
  Movers From Falling Asleep, From
  Falling Asleep Union

m Clock Winders Union

GROUP IV—Left to right
Make-Up Men In Charge Of Patting Star's
  Face But No Lower Union

Make-Up Men In Charge Of Patting Star's
  Shoulder But No Higher Union

Neck Patters Union

Yes-Men In Charge Of Making A Circle
  With Forefinger And Thumb To Tell
  Star How Great He Was Union

Backstage Dust-Blowers Union
  (This is a dock worker who got the
  job for no other reason than to
  prove to Management how powerful
  The Longshoremen's Union is)

CHAPTER 5

KNOW YOUR UNION

The chart below shows the "Chain of Command" of a typical Union:
The dotted lines show the efficient flow of authority, and
the black arrows show the efficient flow of disappearing funds.

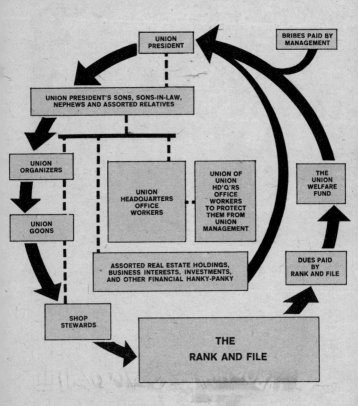

CHAPTER 6

FUTURE GOALS OF THE LABOR MOVEMENT

Following is only a partial list of the wonderful goals that Organized Labor hopes to attain in the near future:

● To Unionize ALL workers in the nation, and to see to it that those who refuse to join Unions DON'T WORK! In this way, workers will help Labor fight the cruel, dictatorial practices of Management.

● To set up a minimum wage standard of $50 an hour for workers—with a lot higher wage rate for *skilled* labor.

● To cut the work week to 4½ hours in order to give Union members more free time to spend with their safety deposit boxes.

● To set up a system of free medical care, hospitalization and retirement benefits for valets and butlers of Labor Union Leaders.

● To strike defense plants only under the following two circumstances: When there is no national emergency—and when there is.

● To provide decent working conditions, liberal pension plans, and fair take-home pay for all Bosses, regardless of race, creed or color.

CHAPTER 7

THE WONDERFUL, GOD-GIVEN RIGHT TO STRIKE

TOO OFTEN THESE DAYS, Management is heard to complain about unnecessary and costly strikes by Labor. This is sheer stupidity and selfishness on their part. There are *no* unnecessary strikes! All strikes are fair and healthy for the economic structure of the nation. On this page, and the remaining 167 pages that follow, we would like to explain the tremendous importance of strikes, and show how they are helping to etaoinshrdlu

DUE TO A SUDDEN, UNNECESSARY AND COSTLY STRIKE BY THE LABOR MANUAL TYPOGRAPHERS UNION, AND THE LABOR MANUAL PRINTERS UNION, WE ARE UNABLE TO COMPLETE THIS HANDBOOK   FURNDOC RUBBER STAMP CO.

THE SUNDAY DRIVE

55

A MAD LOOK AT

60

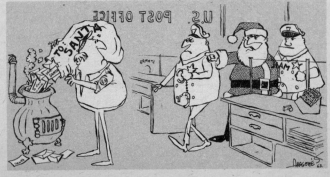

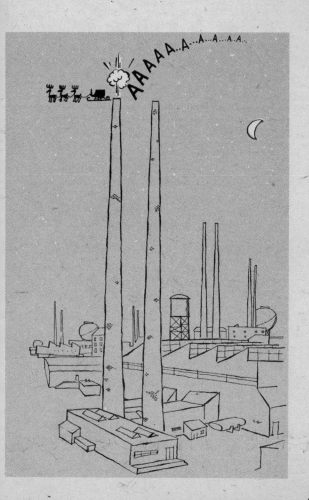

Jabber-Whacky

or

ON DREAMING, AFTER FALLING

ASLEEP WATCHING TV

WRITER: ISABELLE DI CAPRIO

ARTIST: GEORGE WOODBRIDGE

66

'Twas Brillo, and the G.E. Stoves,
    Did Procter-Gamble in the Glade;
All Pillsbury were the Taystee loaves,
    And in a Minute Maid.

Beware the Station-Break, my son!
    The voice that lulls, the ads that vex!
Beware the Doctors Claim, and shun
    That horror called Brand-X!"

He took his Q-Tip'd swab in hand;
    Long time the Tension Headache fought—
So Dristan he by a Mercury,
    And Bayer-break'd in thought.

And as in Bufferin Gulf he stood,
    The Station-Break, with Rise of Tame,
Came Wisking through the Pride-hazed wood,
    And Creme-Rinsed as it came!

Buy one! Buy two! We're almost through!
    The Q-Tip'd Dash went Spic and Span!
He Tide Air-Wick, and with Bisquick
    Went Aero-Waxing Ban.

And hast thou Dreft the Station-Break?
    Ajax the Breck, Excedrin boy!
Oh, Fab wash day, Cashmere Bouquet!"
    He Handi-Wrapped with Joy.

'Twas Brillo, and the G.E. Stoves,
    Did Procter-Gamble in the Glade;
All Pillsbury were the Taystee loaves,
    And in a Minute Maid.

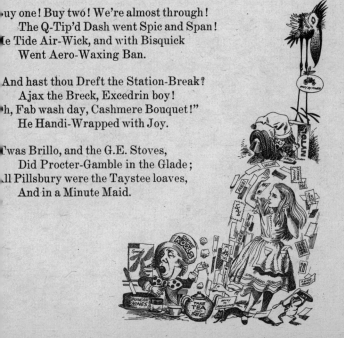

Every year, the movie industry makes a big hoo-hah over the Academy Award
Frankly, we're not impressed. How tough is it to make a movie when you hav
$37,000,000 to blow on it? Huh? MAD feels that it's about time the real
dedicated movie-makers of this country get their deserved recognition! W
mean that vast army of amateurs who are devoted to the cinematic art despi
limited funds and even more limited talent . . . the "Home Movie Makers"! An
so, in order to give 'em what's coming to 'em, MAD Magazine proudly present

From the fabulous Knotty Pine Basement in the garishly furnished split level house of Mr. Louis Kreevitch, overlooking the other eleven thousand two hundred and fifty-seven garishly furnished split level houses in lovely Levittown, New York—the "Home Movie" Capital of the World—the Amateur Motion Picture Academy of Arts and Sciences presents "The First Annual Academy Awards Ceremony"!

Out of more than 1,796,542 reels of film submitted, the Academy has chosen the on it considers to be the finest examples of the "Home Movie-Making Art". To supervis the balloting, the Academy has engaged th services of Mr. Irving Waterhouse, famous candy store owner, who is also a Notary Public, and took two years of bookkeeping at Rutgers night extension school. He will hand me the envelopes, which have been sealed with library paste, and I will open them and read the nominees and winner i each of the categories . . .

KINDA SLOW AREN'T YA, PAL?

The ACADEMY AWARDS for
HOME MOVIES

Our projectionist, Mr. Lyman Fumbler, will show excerpts from each award-winning film. Since Lyman always has a little trouble threading the film, I'd like to ask you not to stamp, whistle, or clap your hands in unison. Also please refrain from making shadow pictures of swans on the screen! That means you, too, Mr. Waterhouse! Well, I see that Lyman is about ready—so—on with the Awards . . . !

THE MARVIN

ARTIST: MORT DRUCKER

WRITER: STAN HART

The first category is for **"Best Coyness"**! The nominees are the films: **"Aw, C'mon, Uncle Jack"**, featuring Jack Gluck being coaxed to do his 'Pat Rooney imitation'—

"Girl of 4, Where Are You?" with Diane Picknoze doing "I'm A Little Teapot" while sitting under a piano—

"Modesty", starring Theresa ▮ reluctantly yielding to press▮ to show her new engagement r▮

And the winner is Mrs. Selma Needleman for her great performance in "Oh, please—Don't—I look Terrible!"

Congratulations, Mrs. Needleman! To you goes the Academy's Award Statuette . . . "The Marvin"!

Oh, I'm so surprised, I can't talk . . . so I'll just hand out these mimeographed copies of my modest acceptance speech!

72

And the winner is: **"Goodbye, Already"**, starring Claude Fibula on location at the Long Island Railroad Depot—

I'd like to give thanks to all the people without whose efforts, I would not be here tonight—to Dr. F. Lawson, a giant among bone specialists . . . to Lincoln Fram, the greatest X-ray technician a guy was ever blessed with . . . to insurance man Albert S. Alexander, a claim examiner's claim examiner . . . and last but not least, to lawyer Sam Leighton for his invaluable behind-the-scenes work on my million dollar negligence suit . . . Thank you, one and all!

For the best "Special Events—Wedding" category, nominees are: "How Romantic", with Aunt Ida and Aunt Zelda waltzing together at Shirley Plutz's wedding . . .

"Just What We Wanted", featuring Fran and Walt Akers opening their presents, with the bride's mother calculating what each guest spent—

"Unidentified Flying Objects", with the kid brothers of the happy couple throwing shelled peanuts and scalin mint patties across the dance floor–

And the winner is: **"Eat, Darling!"**, showing how adorable it is for a grown man to get fed like an infant . . .

The "Marvin" goes to Jerry and Ginny De Fuccio! However, a slight technicality prevents the Academy from presenting the Award until their community property settlement is agreed upon!

Now the award for **"Priceless Memories Of Children's Parties"**. The first nominee is **"The Search"**, a candid study of the innocent joys of childhood . . .

Joan Fagel's film, **"You're Driving Me To An Early Grave"**, starring her twins poking each other in their unending "I-Got-You-Last!" contest—

"The Actress", with Clara Engleha attracting attention by performi her 'Make-Believe-I'm-Dead' routi

And the winner is: "A Boy's Best Friend Is His Dog, But Not On His First Birthday", with fiendish Donny Portnoy—

Accepting the award for Donny is his father, Eric Portnoy . . .

Thank you—and I know that Donny would want me to give credit to that late great canine showman . . . the immortal Fluffy, whose memory will serve as an inspiration to us all!

The nominees for the **"He's Funny Enough To Be On TV"** category are: **"Diamond Lil"**, with Lenny Rupp dressed as Mae West, embarrassing his family for 50 feet of film—

"Girl Overboard!" featuring horseplay by Harry Hartnett as he gaily throws his terrified date into the pool, knowing full well she can't swim—

"The 65th Birthday", starring Car— Bletch doing his clever 'This Food Stinks!' pantomime at the catere— party his son gave in his honor—

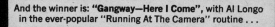

79

In the **"Pictures Of Our Trip"** category, the nominees are: **"State Straddling"**, Renee Abbott's amazing documentary on how one State borders on another . . . .

"A Great Bunch Of Guys", the film Frank Leemy runs for his relatives—showing people they don't know, and whom Frank will never see again . . .

"Golden Gate City—I Hear Your Heartbeat", Larry Mack's arty film essay of San Francisco as seen through his wife Babe's armpit . . .

And the winner is: **"Driving Across America, Land Of Scenic Splendor"**, Doris Flang's classic example of how to shoot an entire travel film through a moving car's windshield—

Thank you! And I want to thank my husband whose driving helped make our trip from New York to California the happiest 13 hours in my life!

And that brings to a close the **First Annual Academy Awards For Home Movies.** The winners will celebrate at a lavish party in the two rear booths of Mr. Waterhouse's candy store. And . . . please, winners! No movie cameras! We want to enjoy ourselves!!

SPY

VS

SPY

Every year, 1 out of 3 families has someone in the hospital. In case you haven't made it in the past 2 years, we don't want you to be ignorant when you make it this year. Since you probably believe you know how hospitals work from watching TV (which is typical of your muddled thinking!), we'd like to clear the air with

THE
MAD
HOSPITAL
PRIMER

ARTIST: GEORGE WOODBRIDGE   WRITER: STAN HART

Lesson 1

ENTERING THE HOSPITAL

See the Emergency Room.
See the patient who has just arrived.
See him lying beside the Admitting Desk.
See him writhing in pain.
Oooooh! Owwwww! Oyyyye!
Medical science cannot help him.
Medical science cannot relieve his suffering.
Not until he produces his Blue Cross Card!

Lesson 2

THE HOSPITAL ROOM

See the hospital room.
See all the clean white sheets.
Why are they over one patient's face?

See the hospital bed.
See the nurse crank it up.
It bends in the middle.
The patient in it wishes he could
      bend in the middle.
Mainly because he is lying on his stomach.

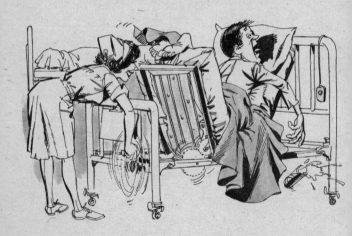

Try and find a comfortable position.
Twist! Turn! Scrunch!
There's a patient who has found a
      comfortable position.
He is in traction.

See the button near the bed.
Try pressing the button.
Nothing will happen.
What is the button for?
Maybe it lights up the Christmas tree
      on the White House lawn.

Lesson 3

BEFORE THE OPERATION

See the patient on the night before his operation.
The doctor tells him to relax.
He says, "Get your mind off it! Watch TV!"
The patient watches "Ben Casey."
The patient watches "Dr. Kildare."
He watches them perform operations
        exactly like his—
Unsuccessfully.

The nurse gives the patient
        an injection to make him sleep.
But he cannot sleep.
Is it anxiety? Is it tension?
No, it is his backside.
The injection hurts too much to let him sleep.

Lesson 4

THE OPERATING ROOM

See the patient on "Opening Day."
He is awakened at 6 A.M. for his operation.
Operations always take place in the morning.
Afternoons are reserved for funerals.

In the operating room, everyone wears a mask.
This prevents infections.
This also prevents the patient from discovering
that his doctor overslept and didn't show up.
A 3rd year medical student will perform the operation instead.
See how nervous the patient gets just because the doctor asks,
"Is the appendix on the right side . . . or the left side?"

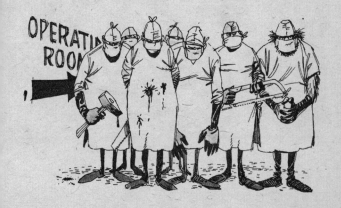

Lesson 5

THE OPERATION

See the surgeon.
See how careful he operates.
He is a dedicated doctor.
He is also a smart doctor.
He knows a dead man cannot write a check.

See how fast the doctor works.
Why does the dedicated doctor work so fast?
He is late for his golf game.
Soon he will stitch up the patient.
Years ago they used regular stitches.
But those hurt when they were removed.
Today they use dissolving stitches.
These hurt when they dissolve.

Lesson 6

THE WAITING ROOM

See the waiting room.
See the patient's family in the waiting room.
Feel their tension during the operation.
At last the doctor comes out.
He announces, "The appendix operation was a success!"
See the patient's family start to cry.
Why are they crying?
Is it because their tension is relieved?
No, it is because the patient entered the hospital
      for a gall bladder operation.

Lesson 7

THE NURSES

See the overcrowded hospital.
See all the people in the corridors waiting for beds.
It is important to get these people beds.
They have just come from the operating room.

See the busy nurses.
Busy, busy, busy.
Nurses are wonderful people.
They are very democratic.
Nurses don't care about a person's color
Or his nationality, or his religion.
They ignore everybody.
Sometimes a rich person hires a private nurse.
The private nurse's job is easier.
She has only one person to ignore.

Lesson 8

THE HOSPITAL FOOD

Hospitals are noted for perfectly balanced meals.
On the one hand, no grease.
On the other hand, no taste.
You can play "fun games" with hospital food.
Games like "Fish or Fowl."
It is simple to play.
Just close your eyes, take a bite, and guess—
Was it fish or fowl?
Usually, it is hash.
So you're right either way.

Lesson 9

THE VISITORS

See all the visitors.
They sit on the patient's bed.
They eat all his cookies.
They make light, carefree talk.
With each other.
The patient wishes the visitors would talk to him.
But they won't. They are visiting
       the patient in the next bed.

Sometimes the fellows from the office drop in.
They try to cheer up the patient.
They tell him not to worry about business.
They tell him that his assistant is doing a great job.
Everyone at the office sends regards.
Except the boss.
He doen't realize the patient has not been at work.

Soon, the nurses tell the visitors to leave.
They are tiring the patients.
How can she tell.
They have all begun to cry.

Dave Berg never went to college. We could say he attended the College of Hard Knocks, graduating Summa Cum Loudmouth, but it'd be an old joke. Then again, Dave is an old joke. Anyway, the author of the forthcoming "MAD's Dave Berg Looks at the U.S.A." now turns his envious attentions to

WRITER & ARTIST:
DAVID BERG

THE
LIGHTER
SIDE OF

THE COLLEGE CROWD

Hey! Mike! Whatchya doin?

Cramming for my exams tomorrow!

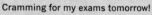

101

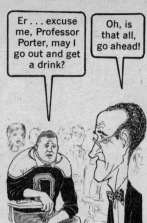

Will you put out the lights, already? All night long, study, study, study! When the heck do you sleep?

My Judy is away at college. She's overwhelmed with courses, studying, term papers, exams—besides leading a very active social life, what with dates, fraternity dances, rallies, football games, sorority rushing...

And yet, this wonderful child still manages, somehow, to find time to write to her parents regularly, like clockwork. And such long, detailed letters, full of emotion...

Really? What does she **say?**

"I'M BROKE! SEND MONEY!"

108

You gotta say one thing about College! It separates the **men** from the **boys!**

Yes! The **boys** go to **College!**

AN EARLY MORNING BATHROOM SCENE

112

114

You marvelled at the ingenious business methods employed by "MAD's Movie Theater Owner of the Year." You cheered for the merchandising tricks used by "MAD's Discount Center Owner of the Year." Now, get nauseous over . . .

MAD'S CHINESE RESTAURANT OWNER OF THE YEAR

ARTIST: JOE ORLANDO   **WRITER: LARRY SIEGEL**

No, Mr. Cash, I am **Walter Crankcase,** not David Berg! And I have something a little **different** in mind!
First of all, I'd like to compliment you on the way you picked up **English!** How long have you **been** in this country?
Forty-nine years next Thursday! Oh, what's the sense of bugging **you** with the phony accent bit! I use it in the restaurant because the **public** digs it! For some reason, it helps business! C'mon in!

This place is certainly a monument to **gaudiness** and **bad taste**, Mr. Cash! Doesn't having this pile of junk as decorations ever get you into trouble with the **Fire Department Inspectors**?

I couldn't tell you! The Fire Inspectors can never get through to **bother** me! That's because there are always so many **Health Dept. Inspectors** lined up to give me summonses for my **F O O D !**

Don't your guests resent all these pictures of **China** on the walls? After all, you **know** the situation between us and the **Chinese Mainland!**

But these **aren't** pictures of China! These are pictures of **Formosa**! As long as we Chinese Restaurant owners play up **Formosa**, we can get away with **anything**!

F'rinstance, how about these post cards with sexy Formosan **girls** on them? They sell like wildfire! They're ten times more profitable than those ridiculous **lichee nuts** we used to peddle in the old days!

It also says they don't serve Column A on **week-days, and weekends!** What's today?
Let's order a **"Family Dinner For Five"**—and **split it six ways!!** Hmmm! Under "Family Dinner For Five" it says "See Family Dinner For Five-to-be-Split-Six-Ways!"
Under "Family Dinner For Five-to-be-Split-Six-Ways" it says **"Don't be a wise guy! There's a $2.50 charge for an extra plate!"**
Listen, we're all **hungry!** Let's order a **"Family Dinner For Seven"** and be **done** with it!
Hold it! It says "You cannot order a 'Family Dinner For Seven' if you're from **different families!"**

Chicken Chow Mein! What else? **Everything** we serve here is Chicken Chow Mein in **one** form or another! These idiots can't tell the difference!

Say, that waiter over there is **pretty rude,** Mr. Cash! He's picking up the **dishes** before the guests have finished **eating!**

Naturally, Walter! If we let customers dawdle over half-finished plates, they're liable to start squashing **cigarette butts** in the food! Then how can we **re-use the left-overs in new orders?**

You're in luck, Mr. Cash! Whenever a **Chinese** family eats in a Chinese Restaurant, it convinces the American customers that the food is **first-rate**! How did you manage to lure that Chinese family in?

There was no problem with that family! It's **mine**! I have them eat all their meals here! In fact, we live right here in the rear of the restaurant! Later tonight, that **table** they're at opens into a large **bed**! C'mon! I'll show you my very profitable **"Take-Out-Order Department!"**

126

127

That **is** an unusual request, Walter! And I must say, you've got **courage!** Very well! Just list your next of kin and sign this form releasing me personally from any liability for **damages** you may suffer—like to your stomach or any of your senses . . .

Wh-wh-where am I? S-some water, please!

Here! Take tea! It's cheaper!!

You're a **courageous man**, Mr. Crankcase! Even the **Health Dept. Inspectors** never had the guts to come **this far**!

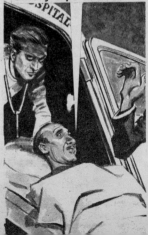

Before I leave, Mr. Cash, please tell me one thing: How can you afford the **up-keep** on such a fancy place like this? Isn't it awfully **expensive to run**?

Not really! We get all our fixtures, decor, furniture and food **very cheap!** You see, it's all **made in Japan! Everything** here is made in Japan! Take me! Even **I'm** made in Japan! I'm **really Japanese!** Americans can never tell the difference! Well, thanks for dropping in —and **SAYONARA!!**

FUNNY PITCHES DEPT.

It's a fact that more people read the comic strips than any other feature in the daily newspapers. Why is this? Because most people don't *understand* them other features! For this reason, famous cartoonists are now being hired by worthy organizations to produce comic pamphlets with important messages. These organizations figure that if someone like Dr. Salk explains how necessary it is to

This pamphlet is put out by the N. Y. State Department of Mental Hygiene, and explains how very important good mental health is to our daily living.

Well, we don't know how successful these comic pamphlets have been for educational purposes, but we do know where a trend like this can lead if we're not careful. Mainly, we may be seeing these . .

ARTIST: WALLACE WOOD

WRITER: LARRY SIEGEL

take polio shots, nobody will understand him, but if Little Orphan Annie explains it, the whole thing will make sense. Obviously, they feel that the masses cannot identify with a distinguished scientist, but they *can* identify with an ageless, glassy-eyed idiot. Anyway, here are a few comic pamphlets recently published by non-profit and government organizations:

This one is issued by the U.S. Dept. of Health, Education and Welfare, and shows the necessity of establishing sensible TV viewing habits for kids.

This comic book pamphlet is published by the Planned Parenthood Federation of America, and illustrates the value of planning a family intelligently.

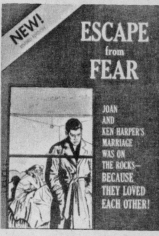

EDUCATIONAL PAMPHLETS

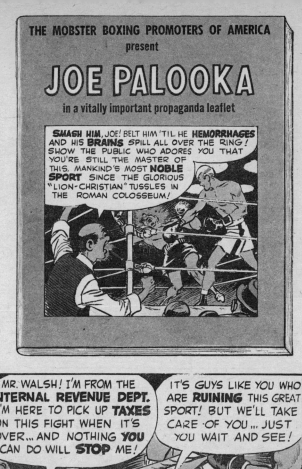

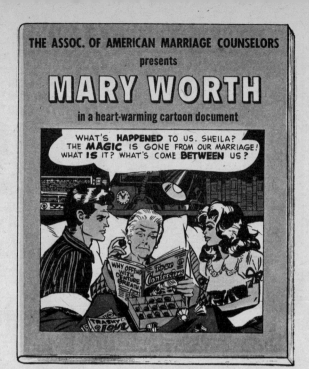

144

"The lively crowd . . . today agrees . . . those who think young . . . say Pepsi, please!"
Sound familiar? Sure, it's the famous singing TV commercial for Pepsi Cola. But did
you know that it was adapted from a popular old song—mainly, Gus Kahn's "Makin'

FUTURE

SINGING

If RALEIGH adapted Lerner and Loewe's

It's arrived, Dear—
That wonderful gift
that we smoked and
saved for so long!

I'm so
happy,
I could
sing . . .

Whoopee"? Well, if we know how the creative minds on Madison Avenue work, it won't be long before more and more singing commercials will be adapted from popular old songs. So, to sicken you before they do, here is our special MAD preview of . . .

TV COMMERCIALS

ADAPTED FROM THE WORKS
OF FAMOUS SONGWRITERS

"On The Street Where You Live"

We have never owned
        a stuffed moose before,
For a stuffed moose we just
        never had no use before;
Now we've thirty-three—
Raleigh sent them free!
We just love all those gifts
        that they give!

People stop and stare
    at our landing strip;
It took fifty million coupons
    to gain ownership;
Raleigh sent it free
With a warranty!
We just love all those gifts
    that they give!

And, oh, just look at our ceiling—
You will see a chimpanzee, too!
We love the glorious feeling
That we're saving up to get him The Bronx Zoo!

Bewitched, Bothered and Bewildered"

I ache again;
I shake again;
My head feels like it's
    sure to break again!
Distressed, dismal and
    despondent
Am I!

My brain again
Feels pain again
Like being smashed in
    by a train again!
Distressed, dismal and
    despondent
Am I!

BLAM

There's one thing
That I'm using—
And it works
Fast—Fast—FAST!

I cheer again;
It's clear again
That Anacin saved
    my career again!
Distressed, dismal
    and despondent
No more!

BOSS

Give us some suds that are long lasting suds
That will slosh through our wash till it's clean!

Buy *Dash* and try *Dash*, 'cause when you apply *Dash*
The dirt on the shirt can't be seen!

We've got the suds that will clean all your duds
But that still won't clog up your machine!!—Ohhhh!

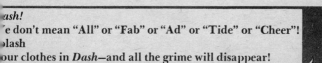

ash!
'e don't mean "All" or "Fab" or "Ad" or "Tide" or "Cheer"!
lash
our clothes in *Dash*—and all the grime will disappear!

"Give My Regards To Broadway"

We bring regards from *Allstate*—
The company that understands!
You've got our new Home Owner's policy,
Which means you're in good hands!

Now that your house is burning,
We know you need financial aid!
We bring regards from old *Allstate*
To say your pre-mi-um's not paid!

Hey! You still using that **greasy kid stuff?**

You ought to use *Vitalis!*
It makes your hair look keen!
That greasy kid stuff that you use
Smells worse than kerosene!

"The Last Time I Saw Paris"

Leonard Bernstein's "The Jets' Song"

THE FIRE
at the ART MUSEUM

Back in September, 1960, we ran a magazine aimed at what we then thought was the most miserable animal in existence—The Beatnik. But in September, 1962, we came up with a magazine aimed even a lower species of the human race—The Racketeer. Frankly, we thought we'd hit bottom. But recently, after digging among the very dregs of humanity, we came up with the individual who is now considered to be the lowest creature of them all by the American public. Here then is MAD's version of a magazine aimed at the . . .

I ATTENDED A P.T.A. MEETING—AND LIVED! By 8th Grade Advisor: Emma Glonk

MODERN TEACHER

A publication for members of the Teaching Profession—sold at a price teachers can afford:

FREE

NOVEMBER, 1963

MODERN-DAY TEACHER ENTERING ON A MODERN-DAY CLASSROOM WHEN HALF RELIGIOUS HOLIDAY WHEN THE STUDENTS ARE ABSENT

IN THIS ISSUE

HOW TO HANDLE PROBLEM STUDENTS

Mainly, Those Who Study Hard, Pass Exams, And Show A Desire To Learn

TEN BATTLE-SCARRED VETERAN TEACHERS DESCRIBE THEIR HARROWING COMBAT EXPERIENCES WHILE SERVING ON HALL-DUTY

With 12 Blood-Curdling Photos.

A FAMED EDUCATOR WRITES
ON CORPORAL PUNISHMENT:

"Before Hitting Them,
Children Should First Try
To Reason With Teachers'"

EXCLUSIVE

SEVEN EASY-TO-RECITE
BLACK MARKET PRAYERS
YOU CAN SNEAK INTO
YOUR CLASSROOM

An Outraged Parent Speaks Out:
WHO NEEDS SCHOOL INTEGRATION?
I'LL LEARN MY KIDS AT HOME!

SPECIAL CONTEST FOR HARASSED TEACHERS
Win A Relaxing, All-Expenses-Paid Vacation in South Viet Nam

ARTIST: GEORGE WOODBRIDGE
WRITER: LARRY SIEGEL

CATCH THAT CHEAT!

Why put up with exam-cheaters?
Nip cribbing in the bud—with

RANKIN
REAR-VIEW MIRRORS

These handy rear-view mirrors attach neatly over your eye glass frames to give a clear, unobstructed view of the classroom while you're writing on the blackboard.

ALSO HANDY FOR CATCHING:

Spitball-Throwers   **Smoochers**
Funny-Face-Makers   **Sleepers**
Dirty-Picture-Passers   **Whisperers**

Inkwell Pigtail-Dippers

AND COUNTLESS OTHER BEHIND-YOUR-BACK ACTIVITIES

ON SALE NOW AT YOUR LOCAL OPTOMETRIST

JUST $2.98 for standard eye glass frame attachment

($350.00 if you wear contact lenses)

Have You Been Suspended Lately
For Recommending Communistic
Literature to your Students?

Play It Safe With
SIMON PURE BOOKS

The Simon Pure Publishing Company has re-written hundreds of well-known subversive works so that they meet the patriotic standards of all parents who are members of the DAR, Birch Society, etc. Here are only a few of the books and stories you can order and safely assign to your class *today:*

* **GOLDILOCKS AND THE THREE EAGLES**
  formerly "Goldilocks and the Three Bears"

* **MELVINHOE**
  formerly "Ivanhoe"

* **THE RED, WHITE AND BLUE BADGE OF COURAGE**
  formerly "The Red Badge of Courage"

* **WEST OF EDEN**
  formerly "East of Eden"

* **THE 39 PRAIRIES**
  formerly "The 39 Steps"

Write For Our Free Catalogue

SIMON PURE BOOKS
Box 1776, Philadelphia, Pa.

DEAR PRINCIPAL LUMMOCK

All teachers who have problems are invited to submit them to Principal Lummock in care of this magazine. If you desire a personal reply, kindly enclose a self-addressed stamped envelope. (Note: Since most teachers can't afford a stamp for a self-addressed envelope, Principal Lummock is discontinuing his offer for personal replies with this issue.)

Dear Principal Lummock:

Last Friday, I assigned members of my class to take home the living things in our classroom and care for them over the weekend. You know, the usual stuff: gold-fish, plants, turtles, and things like that. Anyway, one of my bigger pupils took *me* home with him against my will. Frankly, I had a miserable time, but that's beside the point. Wasn't this a terrible thing to do?

B. D.

Charleston, S. C.

It sure was! You distinctly told your class to take home "living things." You are a School Teacher! You call that "living"?

Dear Principal Lummock:

While travelling through Leveltown, Long Island, the other day, I noticed some builders erecting what looked to me like the most ultra-modern, farthest-out, wildest-looking suburban school I had ever come across in my entire life. Am I right? Is this a new suburban school they're putting up in Leveltown?

F.Y.
New York City

No. F.Y., the building you saw will not be a new suburban school. Its architecture is much too wild and abstract for something as dignified as a school. The structure you saw is going to be a church.

Dear Principal Lummock:

I have been told that many Principals these days are not so much interested in the welfare of their teachers and the education of their pupils as they are concerned with being high-powered public relations men and casting favorable images in their communities. How do you feel about this?

R. T.
Detroit, Mich.

Well, I've been shirt-sleeving this subject with my brain-storming assistants over at my Finster Junior High School shop, where I run a tight little ship—and after spit-balling it around the room, we dropped it into the inkwell to see how it stained. Frankly, the whole thing came up ridiculous, rumor-wise.

Dear Principal Lummock:

I have a problem which has been bothering me for several months. I am Principal of the Elisha Cook Junior Junior High School in Hollywood. Last month, I made a brilliant speech at the graduation exercises. Among other things, I said, "As you pick yourself up by your bootstraps and put your nose to the grindstone and your shoulder to the wheel, you must step boldly, but carefully, onto the Frontiers of Life, remembering to keep your head in the clouds and your feet on the ground, or vice versa. . . . "Anyway, for some strange reason, 85% of the graduation class fell asleep during my speech. Can you tell me why?"

C. D.
Los Angeles, Calif.

Z-Z-Z-Z-Z- Z-Z-Z-Z-Z- Z-Z-Z-Z-Z- Z-Z-Z-Z-Z-Z- ZZZ.

Dear Principal Lummock:

Recently, I read a transcript of the brilliant speech given by the Principal of the Elisha Cook Junior Junior High School in Hollywood, to the graduating class last June. How can I get in touch with him? I want to nominate him for Presiding Officer at the Republican National Convention in San Francisco next year.

D. D. E.
Gettysburg, Pa.

Sorry, D.D.E., the Democrats beat you to it and contacted him first.

Dear Principal Lummock:

I am a 6'7" First Grade Teacher at P.S. 37 in Dover, Delaware. As you might well imagine, with the water fountains in the school halls installed about two feet off the floor for the convenience of the small children, it is almost impossible for an adult to take a drink. I used to try bending over, but I wound up with a slipped disc. Anyway, a few weeks ago, I began kneeling on the floor to take a drink. This worked out fine for a few days, until an FBI man stormed in one day and arrested me. Can you tell me why?

E. R.
Dover, Del.

It's very simple. He thought you were praying.

meet... ARNOLD GUMBER
MODERN TEACHER'S
Teacher of the Month

Every month, MODERN TEACHER selects one member of the profession who best typifies the American School Teacher, and shows an average day in his life.

At 7 AM, Gumber puts on a double breasted suit and wide-brimmed hat, sticks a cigar in his mouth, and tells his neighbors he's off to his book-making parlor. They don't know that his respectable job as Bookie is just a front for his real vocation . . . a miserable teacher at P.S. 46.

At 8 AM, Gumber handles his first extra-curricular, non-paying teaching assignment in school basement. P.S. 46, built in 1823, was once infested by rats. But the rats are gone now. The school was too damp and dirty for them.

At 8:45, Gumber goes on school yard duty. While extremely hazardous work (with possible death always imminent), being outdoors gives Gumber a chance to sneak a smoke—something you can't do in school—unless you're a pupil!

From 9:00 to 2:00, Gumber handles many important teaching assignments, such as Cafeteria duty, collecting lunch money, collecting bank books, collecting milk money, and collecting switch blade knives from the pupils. (More dangerous weapons are collected from the pupils by the school's special Bomb Demolition Squad. . . .)

At 2:00, Gumber directs his class in a comedy in the school auditorium. Everyone forgets his lines, and the jokes fall flat. At 3:00, Gumber receives his monthly paycheck backstage. He goes on stage and shows it to the audience. This gets the biggest laugh of the day.

At 3:15, Gumber is picked up by police for authorizing the use of a dirty text book entitled "Improper Fractions." He is fingerprinted and booked. He pleads for a prison term, but since it's his third offense, he receives the maximum penalty. He is sentenced to return to P.S. 46 as a teacher!

THE INQUIRING
TEACHER

QUESTION: How do you feel about teachers going on strike?
WHERE ASKED: At various schools and strike picket lines.

SHIRLEE BRONX
**Fourth Grade Teacher
And Potential Wife**

I don't see why teachers have to resort to something as degrading as strikes. Now take me, for example. I'm an average, conscientious young teacher who lives at 147 Mosholu Parkway, a keen dancer, swell company, and my telephone number is MQ-O-4299.
All I want is to bring education and enlightenment to pupils for the rest of my life (unless I get a better offer, like getting married, say, next Tuesday). I think the $60 a week I get is more than enough and I can live on it very comfortably. Of course, my father, who I live with, and who is also a teacher and has to support me and my mother—*he's* got problems!

JAMES HOFFA
**Labor Union Leader
And Humanitarian**

Sure teachers should go on strike. Everybody should go on strike. Striking is healthy. It takes people out of their houses where they can get into trouble, and puts them on safe street corners. I like to strike. I like to strike all the big companies. I like to strike all the big plants. I'd like to strike Bobby Kennedy. Right inna mouth! Why shouldn't teachers strike? Some of my best friends are truck drivers. Some of my best truck drivers are teachers. When they're not driving trucks. Well, they gotta eat!

176

ROBERT T. WAG

Mayor and Distinguished
Public Servant

I think it's terrible when public employees have to resort to strikes. Look at me, I'm a public employee. You don't see me striking. I do the best I can on my $40,000 a year. And take my Governor friends, they're public employees. They don't strike. Just the other day, Governor Rockefeller swore to me he'd never strike for more money. And President Kennedy told me the same thing. He's a public employee. Recently, the teachers in my city wanted a raise. Did they go on strike? Of course not. We settled the whole problem by talking. That's how you always settle problems—by talking. I sat down and I talked to them. I said, "You're not getting any more money, and that's settled!"

HERMAN KLING

Professional
Failing Student

I'm all for teachers going on strike. After all, they're human. They have a right to a living wage and decent working conditions. If, by going on strike, they bring out into the open the terrible injustice that is being played on one of today's most important professions, then I'm all for it. I'm all for anything that will open the public eyes, that will open the public minds, and that will close the public schools.

177

This Month's Colorful Report Card Terminology

In keeping with the common practice in schools across the nation of disguising the true character and personality of pupils so their parents won't get like a trauma, MODERN TEACHER offers another installment of some new and colorful double-talk terminology for use on report cards.

"He has an unquenchable thirst for spontaneity in education, which has been best slaked by the give-and-take of classroom discussion, as opposed to the sterile atmosphere of a non-scholastic milieu."

TRANSLATION: He hasn't done his homework in three weeks!

* * * *

"While his personal intellectual capacity is limitless, he rarely hesitates to absorb knowledge from others around him in order to enhance his image as a well-rounded pupil."

TRANSLATION: He cheats on exams!

* * * *

"He allows himself the healthy luxury of unleashing his pent-up emotions, which, had he suppressed them, might turn him into a seething cauldron of self-consuming neuroses."

TRANSLATION: He kicks, scratches, bites and spits!

* * * *

"He has an innate desire to examine at firsthand the vicissitudes of life, which has been best satisfied by personal pilgrimages into the very maw of civilization."

TRANSLATION: He cut classes 24 times this term!

* * * *

"He appears to prefer the cloistered atmosphere of solitary study, rather than engage himself in the communication of class discussion."

TRANSLATION: The other kids steer clear of him because he doesn't wash.

* * * *

"He is deeply concerned with the physical well-being of other students, seeing to it that they do not overindulge in calories or harm the calcium content of their teeth."

TRANSLATION: He steals cookies and candy from his classmates.

* * * *

"His is a wandering, probing mind, which by its very nature, should not be accelerated onto new horizons too rapidly, but should be allowed instead to return to areas once before explored for the purpose of gathering additional insight.

TRANSLATION: He's going to be left back this term.

THE EVOLUTION OF THE U.S. TEACHER

A look at how the American Teacher has developed (or to use a better word—deteriorated) over the past century

100 YEARS AGO

Back in 1863, the American Teacher was an unbending figure of authority. He was big and strong, with a large, sinister-looking mustache. His students hated and feared him. But they respected him. His teaching methods were strictly hit or miss. Either he'd hit the pupil — or he'd miss him when he cracked his large whip. But even when he missed, the wind burns that resulted were extremely painful. Life was rough for students in those days, and many of them used to run away . . . down South, in hopes of becoming slaves and living easier lives.

50 YEARS AGO

In 1913, the American Teacher was still a rigid figure of authority, but he wasn't quite as big and strong as his predecessor, and not everybody feared him. For example, heavyweight champion Jack Johnson didn't fear him. (We can't think of anyone else!) He was a lot more liberal in his teaching methods. He abandoned the whip. Instead, his students were taught to the tune of a hickory stick. (We know it doesn't make much sense when you say it, but when you sing it, it sounds great!) Life was still rough for students, and many of them used to quit school to work in factories for 18 hours a day—which was more tolerable.

25 YEARS AGO

In 1938, the Female Teacher came into her own. She was anywhere from 25 to 65 years of age (but she always looked over 100!) She was a lot bigger and stronger than her predecessor, and a little bit uglier. But being students under her was a breeze. She rarely hit them with anything larger than a ruler, and in six months time, students never even felt it any more. But she was still feared and respected, just as if she were a man. And that's because most of her pupils weren't absolutely sure she wasn't!

TODAY

Today, the American Teacher is like a lost chicken wandering across a road, trying to get to the other side. In other words, he is a joke! No one hates him, no one fears him, and no one respects him. They merely tolerate him. Like a cold. He would never dream of belting a pupil with a whip or a hickory stick or a ruler. He has used his fists, though — but only in self defense. However, there are classrooms in the U.S. that are controlled by unbending figures of authority who are big and strong with sinister-looking mustaches whom everybody hates and fears but respects. The trouble is, they're not Teachers . . . they're pupils!

THE MOONLIGHTER'S CLASSIFIED ADS

Help Wanted—Male

CARNIVAL BARKER—9 PM to 1 AM weekdays, all day Sat. and Sun. Good opportunity for Elocution or Speech Teacher. We supply disguise so your students won't recognize you. 50¢ an hr. Write Box 195 MT.

CAR WASHER—Steady part-time work. Prefer Professor, but will accept Junior High School Principal. Must be College Grad. Here's your chance to clean up. Box 84 MT.

CATTLE SLAUGHTERER—Opening for aggressive, husky young Teacher. Chicken-plucking experience helpful but not necessary. 2 AM to 4 AM, Tuesdays and Thursdays. Bring own sledge hammer and knife. Box 14 MT.

PIZZA FLIPPER—We looka for a qualifi Teach. Write to us stronga selling letter anna tell us why you the man for-a this job. Then drop-a by inna few days anna read it to us. Box 57 MT.

SANDHOG—Work in a nice cool tunnel. Ditch-digging experience unnecessary. Free Hosp. Benefits, unless you get like the bends. Must know how to swim underwater. Box 42 MT.

Help Wanted—Female

FRUIT PICKER—Healthy, outdoor work for Teacher in the Rio Grande area. Excel. working conditions, friendly atmosphere, except for occasional hostile wetback attacks. 20¢ an hour and all you can eat. Lemon harvest starts this week. Box 121 MT.

PILLOW STUFFER — Prefer Teacher with M.A. degree. Salary commensurate with pillow-stuffing ability. Excellent opportunity. Can eventually lead to mattress-stuffing for the right woman. Box 34MT.

SANDHOG — Work in a nice cool tunnel. Typing experience unnecessary. Free Hospital Benefits, unless you get like the bends. We know it's crazy advertising for a woman sandhog, but who can tell how desperate you school teacher broads are! Box 42 MT.

WOMAN — Mature, intelligent Teacher preferred. Hard to describe type of job, but rest assured you'll work like a horse. 40¢ an hour. Free Death Benefits and Hay-Break Box 36 MT.

Situations Wanted—Male

BRIGHT, personable, cheery, ambitious, aggressive, friendly, religious, eager Princeton Professor desires part-time job as shirt folder. Am experienced, and have own pins. Box 347 MT.

PHYSICS TEACHER, Rhodes Scholar, gd. friend of W. von Braun, seeks challenging part-time position as bus-boy. Look gd. in uniform. Will relocate to new school if necessary. Box 19.

Apartments To Share—Male

TEACHER, convicted of one of the most fascinating capers in Moonlighting History—Bank Robbery—wants to share comfortable cell with another convicted Moonlighter in same prison. Don't want bird-keeper, self-proclaimed lawyer, or book writer. This place is lousy with them. Box 97 MT.

THE BLACKBOARD JUMBLE

NEWS 'N' GOSSIP ABOUT THE TEACHING PROFESSION

By Harold "Sandy" Wilner

Hats off to industrious Principal Harvey Higgle, of Birchwood Junior High, who is augmenting his income with a clever use of his inter-classroom public address system. Harv personally conducts a swinging 9 A.M. to 3 P.M. disc jockey show of rock 'n' roll records and witty patter—even during exams. He's fully sponsored by local candy stores, ice cream parlors, saloons, burlesque houses, and other business establishments with messages of importance for today's school-age youngsters . . . Bad news for Ruth Bleaker, Third Grade Teacher at P.S. 131. Her parents refused to give her permission to marry one of her pupils. They feel that 31-year-old Donny Thyson is a bit too old for her. Better luck next time, Ruthie . . . Good news for the Henry Peskins in the person of a brand new 7-pound bouncing baby boy. Henry teaches math at the Jack Holt Memorial High School in Beverly Hills. His wife is a former Kindergarten Teacher, who used to conduct the 2 A.M. to Dawn session at the slightly overcrowded P.S. 6.

* * * * *

Best wishes to P.S. 193's Irma Brechwold, who will celebrate her 70th year as a teacher next month. 92-year old Irma, who tried to retire several times in the past but was asked to stay on by school authorities because younger teachers refuse to work for $38 a week, will celebrate the day quietly. Only the immediate family will be present at a small party given in her honor, including her mother, P.S. 193 teacher Maude Brechwold. Reba Brechwold, Irma's grandmother, who sprained her ankle while teaching gym at P.S. 193 last week, will not be able to attend.

* * * * *

Memo to the ridiculously spoiled students at the suburban Arthur Fingerhut School: Free bus service has now been extended to include all pupils who live more than 10 feet from the school. Previously, only pupils who lived 20 feet or more from the school could ride. And now for some bad news, kids: Since your whole school is on one level, the city has turned down your request to install escalators in the building . . . The City Planning Commission of Finnque, Illinois, has just given the green light for a new 4,500 housing unit development to be constructed within a three-block radius of P.S. 238. Naturally, no new school will be built in the area, so P.S. 238 will be a trifle more overcrowded. To make room for the added influx of pupils, all teachers will be asked to stay home on school days.

* * * * *

In the educational battle for survival between the West and Russia, this column has always spoken out strongly for encouraging brilliant students who show promise and are well-advanced for their age. Which is why we were so excited by the card we just received from teacher Herman Fiffnik. Herman tells us that every pupil in his First Grade class speaks flawless French. However, upon investigation, we found out there's a slight catch here. French is the *only* language they speak. Herman teaches in Bordeaux, France. (Can't you ever be serious, Herm?)

* * * * *

Our condolences to the family of heroic Irving Doren, who taught Science at the brand new Richard M. Nixon Junior High School (which was involved in building graft and collapsed last week due to faulty construction). When he noticed that his room was sinking below the basement, Doren allowed his students to abandon class, but he refused to leave his desk. It isn't very often that a teacher is courageous enough to go down with his classroom. We will never forget you, Irv . . . Worried because your students act like a bunch of dolts whenever a Superintendent or Principal drops in unexpectedly to sit in on one of your classes? Here are some excellent questions, submitted by Ninth Grade Teacher Harold Opp, which you can ask safely: "How much is two and two?", "Spell cat!", "Who would like to demonstrate 'breathing' for today's 'Show and Tell'?", "Which of these famous men discovered the Hudson River: (a) Henry Hudson (b) Seymour M. Dopplefinger (c) Paul Anka?" Contributor Opp promises to send along the answers in time for next month's column.

* * * * *

Best of luck to Fifth Grade Teacher Victor Emster, of P.S. 49. He's taking the "Big Step" with his childhood sweetheart, Miriam Troy. The couple will live at the home of Miriam's parents until Victor decides what he wants to do for a living . . . We hear that thousands of letters are pouring into Washington every day, congratulating all the Congressmen who have been successfully fighting Federal Aid to Education. The only trouble is, they're all from Nikita Khrushchev.

* * * * *

Will some of Harry Carruther's friends at City College please do something about helping him to get rid of the terrible inferiority complex he's recently developed? It just isn't dignified for a respectable College Professor to wear one of those idiotic false-nose-and-eye-glasses disguises whenever he goes in to pay his rent. Even though Harry *did* discover that the new landlord of the 57 story apartment building he lives in is Seymour Gribble, whom Harry flunked in Business Administration two years ago.

THE MOONLIGHTER'S PAGE

What's What Among The "Part-Time Job Set"

Along Teacher's Row

The Fourth Annual Teachers Dance at The Potrezebie School last month was a huge success. Biggest joke of the evening was on the strangers who happened into the gym and thought that the affair was a Costume Ball. They didn't know that all those present were actually teachers dressed in the uniforms of the part-time jobs they were headed for . . . after the Dance.

Meet Sylvia Kupp, "Moonlighter Of The Year". Since January, Sylvia has been teaching her class Algebra all wrong . . . intentionally! With poor grades, the students have naturally had to seek help from an outside tutor. So far this year, Sylvia's income has been $3,422 as a Math Teacher, and $22,000 as an outside Math Tutor.

Here's Evelyn Glick, Biology Teacher at The Fink School, and After-Hours Wine-Maker, catching up on some of the part-time work she didn't get a chance to finish the previous night.

SHIP WRECKED